# Rewilding the Soul

# Rewilding the Soul

Hannah Sinead Hogan

Red Tree Press

# CONTENTS

# CONTENTS

For every soul in search of something indefinable, thank you for seeking, may the pieces of my heart help guide you back home.

*Within each of us is each of us*

*yearning to find the other, until*

*deep inside*

*the pages open*

*to remind that we are the story entire*

# Origami Star

I open up some empty Tupperware,
a sandwich box,
                        am I there?
Running out of ideas of places to look
down the back of the sofa
                in my sock drawer
I now only exist in a forlorn scrapbook.
Catching glimpses in every surface I happen to pass,
a foreign reflection
                        the ghost of my own past.

I found an intricate origami star
that I folded once
in a time when I would sit in biology laboratories
learn about maggots,
                        hearts,
                                transpiration in trees.

This is a time that I know I lived
but witness now through a depersonalised haze
drawing on the pathways of this neurological maze
to remind that I was
                and still remain
part of the world,
                still playing the game.

I forget the rules,

sometimes questioning if I ever knew
remembering landscapes I once drew,
plains of my fantasies seem more real to me now
~ constant rain,
                         hurrying figures pass me by,
is this unprevailing tempest simply
a projection of my own mind?
The world around me
               people I see,
striving to locate the best in all,
presented with unrelenting negativity


how is it that I could have gone so very far,
did I disappear with the u n r a v e l l i n g
of an origami star?


If I don't know where I went away
how can I invite myself back out to play?


I checked the panorama of my dreams,
my bookshelf is bare
                         my canvas blank,
it took a while to find where the Mary Rose sank;
destined to founder on an unknown seabed, I am
lost to the seas of my history
unless restored to a museum shelf or
                                        hopefully
just to my own head.


'Wanted' I shall put on my reward-less posters,
I've lost me

my personality
every last defining quality.
                    I've grown into the empty vessel
                    you always said I was
I lost my cargo in a game of dares
that I played with fools whom I knew not to trust,
    I sold my soul
for another powdered day
where life would take all meaning away;
prevail in the moment, soldier on
for another day,
                another week,
                        another month.


But now I've come looking

so where am I?

gone knocking on all the doors inside.
Some of them open,
many do not,
                others fester with emotional rot.
I try to remould my once intricate origami star
try to follow the path of old folds, ones
made whilst sat in a biology laboratory
where I was first learning evolution theory,
folds
made so competently
                    when I was still within reach of me.

# She

She cries behind the tinted glasses
looking outwards,
but rarely in;
She's deafened by her screaming,
failing to quash the inner din

She longs for a state of security
to hold,
to be held;
She's terrified by this prospect,
inadvertently repelled

She wishes to feel something foreign
a warmth,
a tenderness;
She still believes there's hope
beyond that hollow kiss

She tries to uphold a bravado
positivity,
a lie;
She protects herself from the truth
that 'she'
is I

# Testimony

A callous hand makes multiple mistakes
touching, yet I cannot feel
I remember what it is
I ought to feel,
            yet nothing

burning from within
desperately trying to merge with rough skin
scratching at ribs
guiding,
            yet you remain blind

I sigh, a mixture of wanton discontent
and persevering desperation.
You are inside,
outside, all around,

I am lost in your neck
lost to sounds I hear in my head;
Cries for forgiveness, of yearning,
giving myself
                but not for pleasure

for pain, punishment, penalty, perjury

a pretence unto myself that this is what I need.
I want to bleed,

pour out my soul
the damning guilt within
    tossing my hair, I give you what you need

This is my plea,
cry for help;
I bite into your neck,
                muffling
my damning testimony

# Surely

When did I become the human bottle bank
    for everybody's curdled emotions?
        Have I not got enough of my own bottled away?
Now nothing better than the 'come-back-to' girl
when all else has shown you its belly.

I'm the idiot sat waiting with a burnt steak and chips,
                    a re-assuring pat.
It's fine, come back to me, regardless.
I listen,
      I absorb,
            I absolve;
there isn't a problem I can't solve
         unless it's my own.
So come back, hop into bed
I forgive you
        you never left my head.

*We accept the love we think we deserve*
~ Well I must fucking hate myself
so come back,
        fill me with your heartfelt
        meaningful
     temporary
apology
until next time
lay down next to me

link your legs with mine,
there's space for all of you.

But why do you treat no-one else like this?
No-one else is a refuse collector for your unkind actions,
only I take your rejections with a smile on my face
hug at the ready.
Only I am your 'come-back-to' girl
    so surely that means you must love me?

Surely?
*I hate you.*
I know you don't mean it.
*I do.*
    It doesn't matter anyway. I love you.

# Faded Sparks

It's rugged raw riverbed
that ran dry as if overnight,
arid dust bowl that once

upon a different time was
the epitome of life and it's
lack of heartache, the

mysterious disobedience of
tumbleweed emotions,
blowing swiftly away from

me. It's sudden sensation of
loss of that certain sensation;
A singing kettle that once

boiled ferociously in my belly
for your sanctifying words,
is emptied into early morning

coffee with less than luke-
warm inclination. And it's
you and I, perched on

different rungs of ladder,
lying on opposing tree
branches, yet nose to nose,

irriguous breath tap-ta-te-tap
tingling; tickling my
morning dew-dropped lashes.

# The Clock on the Wall

The clock on the wall is
counting down the seconds to
my death. I wonder
how this is possible
with me being dead already

but I have existed between
those two soft hands
moving around me in perfect circles,
a sure sign of insanity
skirting around my circumference,
big to small like there can be

no air to breathe between us

my fingers grip the space tightly
between tick becoming tock
as if to catch the moment
so it can't slip away,
always evading me,
running from today, whereas last week
we simply idled by. From

time to time the hands
they come together, squeezing
out an awkward kiss because this
is our juvenile idea of

moving forwards. No dancing backwards
through minutes

so we weave our way through years,
tripping like tipsy ballerinas
before a blindfolded audience,
the steps are ours
to remember, if only
there was time

for rehearsal. The clock is
sounding out consonants and vowels
repeating my name
so I'm trapped in momentary
illusion that the letters
form words falling from
somebody else's lips, falling
from your lips, but instead it's

just me falling for you, over and over
again. In the time-lapse of the
night sky I see
faces blurred so
features blend and

smiles and frowns become interchangeable,
midday and midnight,
flashing by like my life
in front of pendulum heavy eyes.
Because every time the door bangs shut
and footsteps doppler effect

like fading sirens on flagstones
it's like every other time I died;
with the clock counting down the
seconds until
you walk back into the room
and it starts all over again.

# Hope Springs Eternal

we were at the centre of it all,
the universe, house, bathroom floor,
when hope entered me
harder than a fist clenched
shoved in mouth
to muffle wanton sounds

but softer than freshly baked Camembert.
We sprawled across new terrain
              legs splayed
leaking our need like burst plumbing
                 succumbing
to primal desperation

with truth laid bare on cold tiles
as words dripped from hungry lips,
fierce eyes replied blush of blue candour

trying to guide moments into memories
to later be distinguishable
from the haven
of all my other dissolute dreams

# The Day I Learned to Whistle

The day I learned to whistle
I desperately wanted to share
my pursed lips with your
cathartic cartilage,

> sing it into your ear canal and
> make you vibrate with
> screeching sounds of
> my bowed soul

Rubbing notes across your
arched back;
the violin I'd always
longed to play.

The day I learned to whistle
local vagabond dogs
came tramping down
stark mountainside.

> I momentarily
> became pied piper
> for misplaced creatures

Desperate to retune
shaken memories,
dance as though
dutiful dusk was
coming home late for the first time
known to winter.

The day I learned to whistle
there was no one to
hear me purge
stringed guilt to carrion

                    feasting on that melancholic
                    carcass I fed to
                    the gorging air.

# All of This

I miss you
I love you

There, I said it

words weave together
as we wander apart
unlacing these last ligaments,
prolongating prevailing sinews
and the tearing of my weary, unwavering heart.

Stretched -
A cosmic banded bond
pulled rigid-taut,
my heavy hand held out
with no corresponding tips to touch,
lips rouge-rough
from chewing down
a desperate demanding frown

remembering -
Trying to replicate
the way you tug and release
with soft and urgent need,
my weak and undulating persistent pleading,
bleeding desire
for my Orpheus.

– All of this

Becoming blue and bold,
confident and crisis-stricken.
Blood thins rather than thickens,
thoughts quicken,
nipples, erect lop-sided mountains,
yearning for your heaven
from this
underwhelming underworld I now behold.

– All of this

I miss you
I love you

There, I said it

– All of this

Please linger one merciful moment more
merge your soul with mine,
soft skin sweeping away insecurities
a sanctuary of sensational, inspirational instability,
you floor me
my Orpheus.

For just the tips,
what I would give

– All of this

I miss you
I love you

– All of this

Before we leave
just one more kiss

– This

is all of me.

# Crossing Lines

Fickle glare from sun
shining down against frozen with intent fingers
still frigid numb

shallow breaths panted in tandem
crossing slippery lines in a frosty street
painted as slashes
                        yellow over red

a jaundiced heart ripped open
to pour another drink
one more glass
to never class as a *give way* sign.

But it's time,
once again
I crossed that line

into the realm of the non-sensical;
whimsical line perched precariously on sodden sheets
we sit beneath the multiverse
she smiles another beam
through crooked
                        cracked teeth.
Eating her way through a broken sky
I am set apart
            forlorn in winters' wistful empty park.

Another story, not mine to claim
another song, not for my ears
I hear
     an ego-enhancing tune

set to the entrancing but
already overdue demands
of my frozen frigid hands.

I notice I've crossed the line
one too many times

this time with eager legs yawning
tumbling to the other side, blissfully
empty minds
~ I stumble,
    blinded by the invite of imagined summers'
false hazy rays,
straight back into this city's intoxicating embrace.

The shallow grip I place
as heels dig in,
        another day, another disgrace

another time
I crossed that line.

Compass set to steer me off course
I'm headed out to sea
where curves of each warped wave

wrap around
seep inside every hungry follicle
replenishing stores of lost salt in
tired perspired pores, jaundiced eyes
                              finally dry

and the broken sky pulls me into her
point of perspective
where lips of a golden mouth
caress
          my unbalanced, selfless, vessel of passage;
I yearn for the kiss that would await
on that perpetually unreachable line,
your horizon

the only one I cannot cross tonight.

# Platonic Drift

A tap
        drip drip drips it's final tears

    the well has dried up
and I am empty

no fuel to feed
a hanging basket of browning flowers,
petals crisped and wilted

I wither

with a cracked mask
        zigzagged down the middle,

a fault line
that no amount of time can repair
– pulled apart
        one continent from another

I despair

# Why must you hit me with that stick?

My body is bruised and broken

I have been walking
for a long time

and soles have lost hope;
a lost soul.

Eternal eyes of all the world upon me as I sleep,
no dream goes uninterrupted
there is no escape
from this cutting landscape

as sneers follow, I stumble
- breath held in,
another silent grumble from thwarted onlookers
as I regain posture in agony

So please hand me the stick
as an aid to keep head above water

not to topple,
beat weary legs from beneath me

I strike myself internally
every second I rest restlessly

- trust me
you need not hit me with that stick

that is the one thing
I can still do for myself.

# Coda

I followed you to the end of the earth
just for you to push me off
the void had called
I had withheld

Then

with your forceful encouragement
I succumbed
I became the darkness

And

with a fleeting thought
I realised
I had travelled so far
to see nothing

# ROCK PAPER SCISSORS

It is a game of Rock Paper Scissors
and suddenly I am stone.     You wrapped
yourself around my heart, I couldn't resist
couldn't
        tear myself asunder


unscrewing an inordinately tightened lid
upon a solid jar of stifled emotions, I bore myself
with cowardice
        no place for desire


I can't inspire your feelings anymore and so
I don't know where to take mine, I've heard it
gets better with time,     I dare not believe.


Holding a sieve beneath the tap, watching the
water find a way through ~ it's all you.
Holding
      a palm
above the stove to watch the amber glow, I saw
ripples of red upon desperate skin,
                inner thunder
begins to dampen ~ it's still you.     Trapped,


upon a barbed wire fence,     defenceless, a chicken
before a fox,
      begging is senseless. I am needy.

Besotted. The blood won't clot the way it's meant to,

holding my hand above my heart as the temperature
drops, I am alone
                    my own fault. Guilt stings

hard.        I stare into shallow depths of a pothole in the
road, as if to clamber in, find a new home, I know now
I am alone.
                    Calming

to understand this is where I deserved to land, his
patch of barren earth, hearth without flame. An inane
wish to be far beyond.        Call to me
from the distance, no more restraint to offer, I am

so far past resistance.
          Resilience is a foreign concept, abandoned
on lonely shores,
melted away in that heatwave we created

I am hated by community of mind
destruction has befallen all the voices collecting
to tell me
          This is my doing
                    This is my doing
                              *You* were my undoing

unzip my dress one last time,
          plunge into the pool
          beneath the frozen ice,

I can regain strength in the
bitter emptiness that becomes me, please somebody

hold me. No,
not just anybody
                please
hold me, a pebble against the tide of life

I don't want to be made of stone,
I am
    the rock to which your paper sticks,
I am
    the broken scissors that serrated your soul,
I am
    the pieces of you that made me whole.

# The Skin I'm In

Dappled by the insurmountable passage of time, telling
the story of every last crime I tried to commit
                                to the depths of my memory
                                and forget

the defence against the wars that rage within, the soundproofing
to my ceaseless inner din
        you are the permeable layer toughened by love,
        perpetuating tough love in return
stiffened and scarred by rough love, but
still giving that soft touch in hope that others may learn

The membrane concealing my desire; a shiny veil
                                        stretched oh so tightly
polished off with a film of lust, sprinkling of necessity, layer
of dried glue between
my glee and trust; the forcefield that feeds his tongue,
at the very
            tip of my disgust.

Breaking against weak inner will, cracks form in corners to bare
the story of years
                    the journeys we have ventured upon, a
freckled-based souvenir
for each summer spent beneath our sun

the cuts became whitened marks, intense indents

through furrowed ridges
fraught with overbearing weight of yesterday's screams,
the need to please
etched haphazardly
point of silver scissors hacked
hair from head, came to bed
so many times in desperate hope of a last time


no further glances at the clock, so many final moments that


stretched
into
infinity,


cut through like a ribbon at an inauguration ceremony


serrated teeth in battle to the death, I am
punctured, deflated, maimed
desperate
to acknowledge the person that existed
before I heard my name whispered
in his metallic breath.
A foreigner in chains, clamped tightly
flanked by tethers and zips, whips caress the sign of the cross,
the last drop of holy water
to the forehead; I am never cleansed


filth dries in the creases, crinkled flesh tears open, tears leak from
overflowing reservoirs of hoarded despair,
final resources
swallowed down in depravity, no one left to save me,

turned inside out
it screams

hysteria is written on the surface, blotched drops
of invisible ink stain the screen
blocking out true feelings,
soft and thirsty, parched of that
tender touch,
          I shudder.
The nerves tingling with wanton wishes, semi fulfilled dreams
            shudder,

a caress speaks the volumes that I can't carry
upon my back, words carved into
memory and muscle
clenched, waiting for the moment they tear,
                the feet
hold the residue of all steps taken in vain, along
the very same path
over
    and over
        and over again
tip toe lightly around the elephant in the room,
ripping off the plaster
~ familiar face still hiding there,
           the screams get louder and
the gash deepens
~ you are the straight jacket restraining my inner demons.

Scalding water is no punishment,
        as grim reality of eternity fades

into oblivion
            drops seduce pores, closing up
like dutiful chrysanthemums outside my bedroom window;
they never fail to sleep as sun goes off shift.

I shudder,
            you shudder,
                        we shudder
inside the flawed life jacket I received at birth; you
haven't always been a perfect fit,            I'm
            still growing into you, since you still won't let
me quit.

# Painting Faces

A lick of paint goes a long way,
just consider the sad, sorry state of your own face

when the cracks begin to emerge
cruel veneer allowing blemishes to appear

instead of reapplying an unkept undercoat
revel in beguiling beauty of the unknown.

We're all beautifully broken together so
scrape away to reveal the hidden surface below;

the pooling depths of solid foundation;
brickwork of our souls joined in perfect tessellation.

We are the cosseted and the coveted,
covering, smothering, suffering, suffocating

always painting the truth
with a layer of disdain

strip back to peer into the abyss
brush away final dried pieces

to reveal the naked nature of our shared truth,
a cold canvas waiting to be shown

a mural of love yearning to grow.

# Writer's Block

Creative blockade,
mindless ramblings in brocaded paper
sealing the deal within;
   nothing to say, nothing to think.
Where once was demanding curiosity,
unquenchable thirst
now lies bitter emptiness
  speaking as if rehearsed.

Country walks in affable silence
no longer follow suit
as men and women, strangers, friends
   march in common dispute.
Expressionless faces match memories
of vicious circles,
crippling cycles of hate,
pushing all to the wayside;
  Impervious,
detached.

Hands dropping limply to
lonely sides of legs,
closing gates of mirth,
   locking up the shed;
the sturdy shelter under which
naïve new lovers met,
but fingers let go as animosity grows

      doors are slammed shut
on every embrace.

These plodding people touch their tears
as lakes rise high with pressing fears,
as incomprehensible cranial clutter
      leaves melted minds
where fiction foretells of imaginary crimes.
So glares of sunlight
match stares of detest
forcing stores of resilience to unite,
      coalesce.

So it's time to climb out
of the hole of hallucinations,
magic mirror in hand.
      Peek out through the
machicolations of the inner eye,
pick up your lonely pen
      take a firm,
defensive stand.

# No Competition

Prestigious, the award
of time spent with you
        in receipt
        of time in lieu
I gratefully receive what has been handed out;
handouts are unusual here
as I step forwards to beg
your ultimate prize
I wait a while
palms outstretched to test
struggling, to juggle
a statue of your making;
slender body cast in memories
of density
the absurdity of this

~ how I am still in line to drink another sip

cup leaking
you press a penny into my fist
tell me now, how to resist.
As runner up I only know
to look up
upon
snapped pedestal,

abandoned plinth

smithereens of gleaming trophy
atrophy in my dreams
because I am taller today
than you ever gave credit for,
first place lacks the troth of depth
now offered in my own
healing embrace.

# Carbon Dating

Gliding down like toboggan
on smoothest ice
                              Vaseline lips
caress pimpled flesh as we swerve
oncoming delights.    Rush hour
traffic is stopped in time for strokes

to reverse, retrace tiny steps backwards
across blue cotton on canvas. We

are the multiversal mixed-media duo
collage bursting
across plains with blood, saline, saliva

Eruption of veins and nature's
magic to meld with rains
                    bringing last grains
of desert-painful blizzard onto glue-
smattered ply-board, skyward we look.

Obtuse, translucent, mostly effervescent,
we fizz like sugar sour-drops.
                                        Laces
curling like buzzing electronic wires, we unwind
fingertips and unlock greased lips. Hands

blindly discovering mother nature's

finest,
          particle artwork;
                                    You,
exquisite carbon-based masterpiece.

# Tipping Point

We hang, precarious

on the edge of this precipice
lips pressed firmly together, lungs
barely containing tumultuous weather
legs spread
betwixt which oceans will gather,
waves, they murmur,
heaving
the landscapes' breasts rest
heavy, as heads
hang in dishonour

we hang, precarious

collective carapace of spurious self-confidence
shattered,
throaty thrall of wind
with no kindness left
engulfs us all
as the mouth opens wide
for the kiss of life,
but nothing can thrive in such an environment;

a heart

pumping carbon dioxide and grief.

It is with sweet relief
that we hang,
teetering
on the tip of a moment, gripped
firmly between crumbling teeth,
into the waters we dive, once rich
teeming with life

over the edge we topple
too eager to test how far we can step
before beloved mother
withdraws support for arrogant abuse

all lifelines severed

the pulse beats erratically,

slowing
as this dangerous dance of humanity without humility
denies our hopes
of unity.

The balance shifts
as blood rushes free
blue to red,
reaching up for a new breath

we hang, precarious.

# Breathe

Un-stuff feet from tight new shoes
       wiggling
those timid toes,
develop more room
       to breathe.

A photograph in a dark room
emerging into life,
breathe existence into smiles
on a condensation-based window pane
paint
       glass with frought fingertips, eager to create
lick
       the corners of your mouth
purse
       chapped lips

to mimic
melodic morning chorus
that breathes life's joy into a stiffened, heavy soul;
a tune of birdsong and
concupiscence flowing around wind's gentle curves
to greet you
       when you are alone.

Breathe in
the scent of this morning's
frosty fairground of infinite possibilities,
dreams drip like water
                              helter skeltering down icicles
hanging lazily from trees,
holding up your branches of desire;
breathe,
            transpire.

Heave
the bulk of worries off that hunched back
as you unclasp
unforgivingly clenched hands;
            wiggle
                those appendages
and dance.

Breathe, one - two - three

breathe
            deeply

feel the rhythm of the multiverse coursing through veins;
blood, the red and the blue
hot and cold
            passion and fear
in equal measures
            the fire and the flood,
engulfing you.

Un-stuff feet from tight new shoes
wiggling
           those timid toes
to release rigidity
from your suffering soul.

           Breathe in
to embrace this new day,
               exhale
as you shake these blues away.

# Rewilding the Soul

The roar is pulling through me
    twisting outwards from depths within
control is so limited
with the fear of giving in
to a tide of fetid fury

I will sweep you all away.
Far out on a frozen ocean I will lay you;
icy pillows for weary heads
I am desperate not to slay your dreams

so please stand back
        the floodgates fail me,
arms flailing I hunch in pain
all barriers wrenched away.

Raw
    the taste in my mouth is your blood
but I refuse to feed off this innocence
the cycle must end here
would if I could
but the gaping wound of soul
        meets my physical

the armour is so weakened
by years of brutal betrayal,
dents so deep

plummeting through
each and every time I go to sleep.
Every measure put in place
is in tatters, sinews stretch
    fascia entangles
     the spasm so mangled
there is no release


shattered


I forget how to find a single moment's peace.


The bones rattle,
     the thunder is coming.
I bend over to bellow my wrath
held so dearly for you all,
as close as my most precious child
     I am reviled


Ancestors,
   I am the well of your grief
river of your pain
ocean trench of your longest buried anguish,


the rabid dog within is desperate for his midday sun,
clouds smother me
so with no moon to howl my surrender to
I am unleashed
    into the darkest of nights
where feral,
retching my unwanted truth

projecting my tempestuous torment

I hail down upon this dirt

please collect me in your willowed arms,
help me weep for all the muzzled-mourners
who sowed this path
                    to my potential freedom.

Mama,
        Gaia
see me here
buckled beneath invisible weights of winter's stark savagery
please save me,
let summer come again

as I acquit contorted eons of asperity
torn, disheveled
        but a lighter version of me.

Clearing the skies in time for the first sunrise of spring
my moans are now the
forceful pushing of new birth,
laying to rest that last shard of despair
                            hands plunged deep into earth

I cackle
        a wild woman walking home barefoot
soles sliced but
soothed by mild morning dew

I am unbound
I am born anew.

Hannah Sinead Hogan is a poet, an artist, a singer, a dreamer and a soul-healer.
Not afraid to face the shadows that lurk unloved, she is on a mission to help guide everyone she meets to reconnect with the broken shards of self and stop losing themselves in the ideas of others.
Living a nomadic lifestyle, with a focus on conscious parenting of her spirited young daughter, Hannah has been working through her own tenebrous depths in order to revive the light of her soul in a world that needs illuminating now more than ever.

For more detail about Hannah's life and work please visit www.soultemple.online

9 781739 932404